# THE STUDENT
# ASSISTANCE PROGRAM

# THE STUDENT ASSISTANCE PROGRAM

Tom Griffin
Roger Svendsen

Published January, 1986.

ISBN: 0-89486-350-9

Printed in the United States of America.

Editor's Note:
  Hazelden Educational Materials offers a variety of information on chemical dependency and related areas. Our publica-
tions do not necessarily represent Hazelden or its programs, nor
do they officially speak for any Twelve Step organization.

# TABLE OF CONTENTS

# DEDICATION

Jake Kenyon had a special interest in young people. He demonstrated that interest as a teacher, school administrator, and youth leader. There was much evidence that this interest was reciprocated. After Jake left the traditional academic setting to become an alcoholism counselor and trainer of counselors, he continued to hear from young adults whose lives he had touched.

It troubled Jake to hear that some young people, who were experimenting and perhaps even getting into trouble with drugs and alcohol, were being labeled "alcoholic" or "chemically dependent." Jake did not have his head in the sand; he knew that the label was appropriate for some — that it did not necessarily take 20 or 30 years to become alcoholic or drug dependent. At the same time, he did not adhere to the belief that "a little treatment never hurt anyone," or that early intervention was equated with directing adolescents into A.A. or treatment prematurely.

The Student Assistance Program described in this manual was a special project of Jake's. Its direction and simplicity are due, in part, to his careful attention to a myriad of ideas being discussed, to thoughtful questions he raised, and to sensible suggestions he offered for the form and content of the program.

The project mirrored his own understanding of youth because it calls attention to a multitude of changes going on in an adolescent's life. It challenges adults to hold the young person responsible for behavior in many areas of living — including chemical use or abuse.

Jacob D. Kenyon died of cancer in September 1978 while much of the project was in the planning stages. This manual is dedicated to his memory.

# ACKNOWLEDGMENT

Special recognition and appreciation are extended to Marilyn Brissett and Gordon Grimm of Hazelden for their support and assistance in the development of this manual. In addition, we acknowledge the contribution of Don Weida, Metro Drug Awareness, who is now an Employee Assistance Program advisor at 3M; Paul Dybvig, Minnesota Department of Education; and Ron Brand, Wilder Foundation.

# PREFACE TO SECOND EDITION

In the mid-1970s we began to work with schools in developing student assistance programs. Our work grew from concerns that we shared about young people who were in need of help but somehow were never identified and assisted through their school years. Some school districts tended to deny that students experienced serious family, chemical, or sexual problems. Other school districts acknowledged that problems existed but tended to respond in a legalistic and moralistic style hoping to eliminate troubled students from the schools. Still others developed specific programs designed to help students who were experiencing chemical use problems, suffering from child abuse, or living through family change due to death or divorce. Unfortunately, if students did not meet the criteria for a specific program, they could not receive assistance.

Based on these experiences, we recognized the need for a broadbrush approach to student assistance programs similar to the employee assistance programs.

This Second Edition of the *Student Assistance Program* reflects our original intention plus the past five years of experience in developing, designing, implementing, and monitoring programs in local school districts. Questions and concerns of parents, students, teachers, administrators, and counselors have helped refine some aspects of student assistance programs. Successes, problems, and unanticipated results of these programs have led us to revise our original work.

The most significant observation we have made is that we are really implementing a *student assistance process* in addition to a program. This process is self-correcting, responsive, and relevant to the needs of any particular community. We encourage you to consider your efforts to assist students an ongoing process that requires sensitivity to the changing needs of students, staff, and your community.

Thomas M. Griffin
Roger Svendsen

Minneapolis, Minnesota
1986

# FOREWORD

"Having a student assistance program in a school not only makes it easier to reach kids who are having trouble in school, but also slowly changes the total environment of the school to a more positive one where learning and growth can be rewarding for both students and staff."

— Technical Assistance Consultant
Student Assistance Programs
Area Vocational Technical Institute

"Students bring problems from home and the community to school with them. The school is in a unique position to identify and intervene with students whose problems affect their learning potential or who need outside assistance. The student assistance program allows this to happen through the use of a variety of school/community responses. It works and provides direction for our concerns."

— Coordinator
School Chemical Dependency
Program

"The kinds of things that we have done with students in crisis have been invaluable. We don't react negatively now, and we are able to refer students to the kind of assistance they or their families need."

— Principal

# CHAPTER ONE

## INTRODUCTION

Many students are troubled by problems which interfere not only with their academic and cocurricular performance, but with their emotional, physical, spiritual, and social development as well. And when students are troubled, so are teachers, administrators, counselors, and other support staff. Help is needed — help for those struggling students and for the members of the educational community affected by their struggles.

This book is designed to assist educators to better respond to the students' struggles. It is quickly accepted that those problems and their mishandling hamper the healthy development of the *entire* school community. Consistent, systematic, and professional response to overt as well as covert problems of young people is necessary, and can be provided by school staff without the need for highly specialized training or fear of legal liability. Developing and implementing efforts to help young people resolve their problems and thus open the way for personally and socially satisfying lives must be our shared responsibility.

In this manual, we have tried to raise all the points that must be addressed by any district's concerned constituents: administrators, teachers, support staff, parents, and students. Further, we have tried to offer appropriate guidelines for addressing these points. Each district's policy and program should reflect that particular community. There is no one policy or program of student assistance. However, these guidelines will help you tailor a program that will best serve your students and your community.

**Case Histories: Why a student assistance program is needed and how it can help.**

Tom, a sixth grade student, has been absent without an excuse six times in the last three weeks. He has also been tardy on two other occasions, and the quality of his assignments is poor. Mrs.

Hall, his teacher, is concerned. She calls him in, hoping to discern the nature of the problem. He says nothing is wrong and asks to be excused. Mrs. Hall offers her assistance if he needs it in the future. Behavior remains unchanged.

Mrs. Hall next contacts the nurse, Ms. Axelrod, who is Rice School's assessment person for the student assistance program. Mrs. Hall tells Tom she has arranged a conference for him with the nurse, who is also concerned about his absences and poor school work.

Ms. Axelrod can find nothing physically wrong with Tom, and he is determined to keep "his problem" to himself. However, the nurse turns to another person for assistance with the problem — the school social worker. Mr. Gallaway arranges for a home visit. When he arrives, Tom's mother is intoxicated. In his subsequent interview with Tom, Mr. Gallaway finds out Tom frequently fears leaving his mother because her smoking, coupled with drunkenness, might result in a fire.

The social worker reports back to the school nurse. She meets with Tom for goal setting and to determine a plan of action.

1. **Goal** — Reduce absenteeism and tardiness. **Action** — Ms. Axelrod will arrange a family meeting to increase cooperation and provide assistance to Tom's mother. The student assistance team will provide support for Tom through involvement in a support group and individual counseling.

2. **Goal** — Making new friends. **Action** — Tom will be moved to a classroom where group sharing and circle discussions are a part of the regular classroom.

*Follow up and Evaluation* — Mr. Gallaway will interview Tom and his teachers in two weeks and monthly after that to monitor his behavioral change. Thus help has been given, not only to Tom but his mother, and inappropriate disciplinary action has been avoided.

In another case, in another school, the outcome was not so positive.

Sandy, a seventeen-year-old senior at Brooke High, has been intoxicated at school three days in a row. Several students and at least three teachers noted liquor on her breath, unsteady movements while walking, and argumentativeness both in class and hallways.

Sandy is reported to the principal. Mrs. Drexal calls her in and Sandy responds belligerently to the questions. She is suspended for two days.

The following week she again comes to school intoxicated, and again Mrs. Drexal suspends her, insisting she bring a parent to school with her when she returns three days later.

However, three days later she doesn't return. A call to the home is made, and Mrs. Drexal discovers Sandy has not been home for a day and a night. Her mother tells Mrs. Drexal she suspects Sandy is pregnant and, consequently, has run away fearing the anger of her father. A search for Sandy is futile. Case closed.

Sandy gets no help; her family gets no help; and the staff is not given a chance to practice new behavior which would benefit not only the student and staff but society as a whole.

These two cases, briefly outlined, are patterned after actual cases recorded by school personnel. Rice School's response is enlightened and responsible, has a focus on providing assistance to a student in need, and is productive for all concerned. Unfortunately, Brooke School's response is not directed to the students' needs; it is punitive and results in neither the student nor the family receiving assistance. It is our intention to help you pattern a program of assistance for your students that will help both them and their families. Modeled, in part, after the very effective and comprehensive employee assistance programs actively implemented in many workplaces; the main goal is to systematically and professionally respond to young people's problems as they are manifested in school. More specifically, this model for student assistance has been designed to do the following:

1. Provide assistance to students troubled by physical, emotional, social, legal, sexual, medical, familial, or chemical use problems.

2. Improve the quality of education in schools and the school environment.
3. Utilize existing human resources rather than require new professional staff.
4. Enlist the support and involvement of all professional staff members.
5. Focus on educational concerns rather than attempting to resolve major social problems.

An effective student assistance program will be both comprehensive and realistic. The model presented here attempts to be both.

# CHAPTER TWO

## ADOLESCENTS AND ADOLESCENCE

As those of us working with young people know, adolescence is a time of change, challenge, exploration, and opportunity. It is also a period marked by strong emotions. For some, transition from childhood to adulthood will be constructive and healthy. For others, the attending problems will demand our attention.

Physiological changes that affect size, shape, complexion, emotions, and interests will be noted by adolescents. In particular, their developing sexuality will significantly alter their self-image.

Concurrently, the school environment changes. There is a movement away from self-contained classrooms. Freedom of choice regarding courses and the importance of extra-curricular activities opens new opportunities and new expectations.

At home, the adolescent's place in the family is in flux. The adolescent moves away from a complete acceptance of parental values and begins developing personal values and attitudes. There is an expected and normal pulling away from the family and an increased importance of peers. Tension occurs within the family as both adolescent and parents define new levels of their relationships.

With each change, the adolescent is challenged to develop new coping skills, to develop new patterns of behavior, and to assume greater personal responsibility.

These changes and resulting challenges lead naturally to experimentation with new behaviors, and the emerging self-concept is shaped by these many new experiences.

Some of these experiences will demand more sophisticated decision-making skills than the decisions of just a few years before. The rewards and risks must be weighed, often without personal experience to help. Decisions are made to explore one's sexuality, to explore the effects of chemicals, and to explore one's increasing independence. Risks will be taken, errors will be made, some questions will be answered; but some questions will remain.

Positive opportunities for developing a healthy self-image, for discovering new ways to enjoy life, and for expanding the understanding of life also accompany these risks, challenges, and changes. Unfortunately, errors in judgment will be made on occasion. The severity of these errors will vary from individual to individual. Many students' problems will be less severe than the one confronting Sandy in our case history. However, some students will be faced with even graver problems.

Our task, as caring adults, educators, parents, and friends is to help adolescents utilize all their opportunities to master the tasks of adolescence. We need to help young people recognize and accept the changes that are occurring. We need to help them develop the strengths and skills necessary to confront the challenges of adolescence. We also need to provide young people with the opportunity to explore new relationships and new behaviors in a caring and supportive environment.

The school plays a key role in building this environment and in responding to student problems. Response, prevention, and promotion are the three elements in the comprehensive approach to these problems.

# CHAPTER THREE

## THE ROLE OF THE SCHOOL IN RESPONDING TO STUDENT PROBLEMS

The role of the school includes the responsibility of responding to identified problems, preventing future problems, and promoting positive and healthy behavior. The figure below represents these three goals:

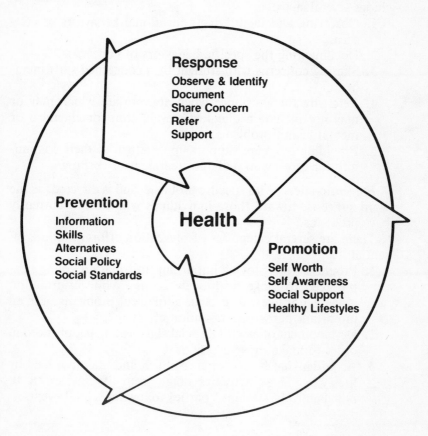

*Response* involves providing assistance to persons and families who are experiencing problems. The primary role of the school in the broad area of response is
* having a process and procedures for identifying and responding to problems among students;
* providing support to the student both during and after the prescribed program, and facilitating a smooth return into the school.

The process of responding to problems within the school includes several steps:
1. Observing and identifying educational behaviors of concern.
2. Documenting the specific behaviors of concern.
3. Sharing concerns with student by a concerned staff member.
4. Referring for assistance when appropriate which may or may not include a diagnostic evaluation for chemical or mental health problems.
5. Providing aftercare support upon return to their community for those who undergo treatment or therapy.

*Prevention* deals with specific problems and is directed, as the word suggests, toward those individuals who do not currently have problems.

There are several categories of prevention efforts that are essential:
1. Programs that provide important information young people need to make healthy decisions. While information alone is not likely to prevent adolescent problems, it is an important part of a prevention effort.
2. Development of essential social skills young people need in order to make those decisions.
3. Activities that help people establish and maintain healthy lifestyles. These activities range from lifetime sports to nonchemical "straight" parties following school events.

4. Social policy measures such as drunk driving laws, drinking age laws, and school policies on the use of tobacco by students, and other regulations which affect behavior.
5. Establishment of standards for safe, healthy, and appropriate behavior within families, social institutions, and the community.

*Health Promotion* is more general and focuses on the healthy development of individuals, rather than responding to specific adolescent problems and concerns. Health promotion is a process in which each person's self-worth is acknowledged and nurtured, while personal and social support are developed and strengthened. Health promotion efforts can be integrated easily into the ongoing curriculum and activities programs of most schools to form the cornerstone of a health program. These efforts include the following:

1. To acknowledge and nurture each person's self-worth independent of performance in an activity
2. To increase self-awareness in students toward an understanding of the feelings and emotions they experience
3. To develop personal, social, and spiritual support systems with strong peer support
4. To focus on healthy lifestyles that include lifelong sports and activities, good nutrition, and stress management

As the necessity increases, each school needs to determine the particular functions it can and will perform as a major contributor to solving students' problems. In other words, what specific steps should school personnel take to create the student assistance program?

# CHAPTER FOUR

## SCHOOL AND COMMUNITY COOPERATION: POLICY DEVELOPMENT

The first step to be taken is policy development based on community needs and concerns including those of the local board of education, school administration, school staff, parents, and students. Thus, representatives from each of these groups should be organized to participate in development of the school policy and administrative procedures necessary to implement a comprehensive and realistic program of response, prevention, and promotion for all students.

In Flowchart I the many facets of policy development are outlined. To simplify the task confronting you, these steps should be used as a guideline for your own school district.

The initial presentation of the student assistance program can be made by anyone within the school or community. However, it is essential that the task force or advisory committee responsible for developing the program include representation from the school administration, teaching staff, support staff, students, and parents. This broad representation will ensure that those persons affected by the program will have the opportunity for input into its development. This will also assure support from these groups in the implementation of the program.

The task force or advisory committee should review and analyze existing school policies and procedures in the areas of chemical use, child abuse and neglect, and discipline. Local needs and resources to meet those needs should be identified to include those of minority populations within the community.

Some school administrators have encouraged the consolidation of many problem-specific policies into one comprehensive student assistance process. For example, the student who is inattentive in class and does poor academic work may be experiencing a family problem, relationship problem, chemical use

11

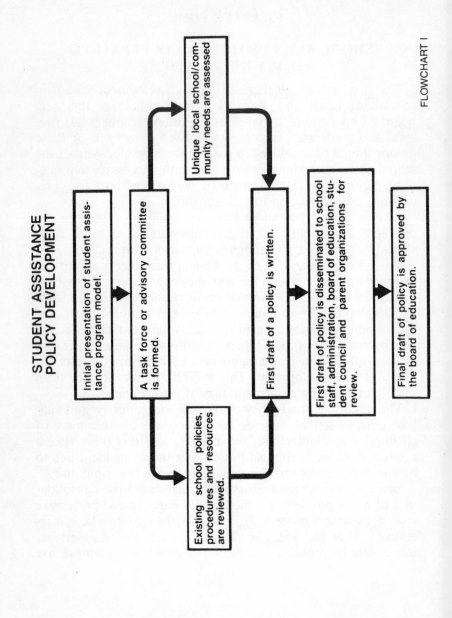

## STUDENT ASSISTANCE
## POLICY DEVELOPMENT

Initial presentation of student assistance program model.

A task force or advisory committee is formed.

Unique local school/community needs are assessed.

Existing school policies, procedures and resources are reviewed.

First draft of a policy is written.

First draft of policy is disseminated to school staff, administration, board of education, student council and parent organizations for review.

Final draft of policy is approved by the board of education.

FLOWCHART I

12

problem, learning disability, or a physical problem such as poor eyesight. Regardless of the cause for the behavior problem; policies and procedures can be developed that give direction to the classroom teacher, coach, or other concerned person for helping the student. None of the problems mentioned above requires a unique policy or set of procedures, special forms, or inservice training. Instead a broad enough student assistance program policy can be developed to allow educators to understand their roles and responsibilities to help students experiencing *any* problem.

Administrators who have consolidated policies and procedures have greatly reduced the need for specialized inservice training for staff on child abuse, chemical use, special education, discipline, and sexual abuse. While these problems may need to be handled differently by preassessment staff, the behavior initially generating concern can be addressed in a systematic and consistent manner by all staff. This also reduces the amount of staff confusion that often exists over the "need to be experts in everything, but what we were hired to do, that is, to teach."

Once the task force or advisory committee has completed this review and analyzed existing policies, needs, and resources, the first draft of a policy defining the role of the school in minimizing student problems should be written. The first draft is then disseminated to all school staff, administration, the board of education, student council, and appropriate parent organizations or associations, for review and input. This process is designed to communicate what is being developed to all persons who will be affected by the student assistance program, and to solicit their input prior to board of education approval of the final policy.

In most situations, if this process is closely followed, the adoption of the final policy by the board of education is a formality, because the necessary support communication and input has been gathered previously.

After the final draft of the school policy has been approved by the board of education, you are ready to structure the student assistance program to meet your school's or district's particular needs as determined by the task force that developed the policy. Flowchart II provides an overview of that structure.

We want to emphasize that within the overall framework, particular program procedures will vary from one school to another due to a variety of factors: community standards and customs, availability of skilled human service resources, and school patterns of organization and management. However, the following are six necessary points of concern in the development of every school's program procedures. These points are carefully defined in the next chapter.

## POINTS OF CONCERN

1. Interaction among educators, other staff, parents, students, and interested community members.
2. Interaction between educators, other concerned staff, and students.
3. Interaction between staff and student assistance preassessment person(s).
4. Interaction between student and student assistance preassessment person.
5. Interaction among student assistance preassessment team members.
6. Interaction of student with the rest of the school community.

# STUDENT ASSISTANCE
## PROGRAM IMPLEMENTATION

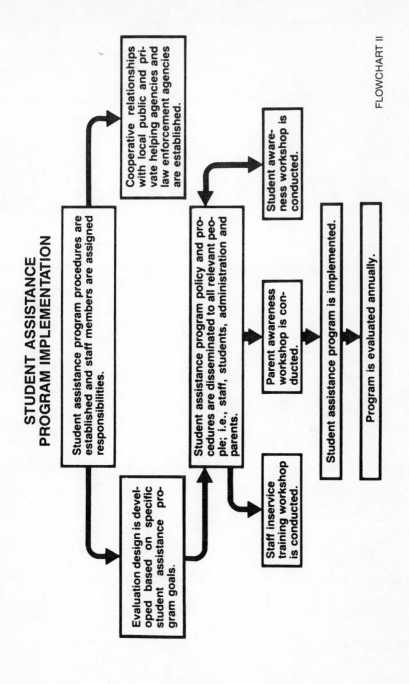

Student assistance program procedures are established and staff members are assigned responsibilities.

Cooperative relationships with local public and private helping agencies and law enforcement agencies are established.

Evaluation design is developed based on specific student assistance program goals.

Student assistance program policy and procedures are disseminated to all relevant people; i.e., staff, students, administration and parents.

Student awareness workshop is conducted.

Staff inservice training workshop is conducted.

Parent awareness workshop is conducted.

Student assistance program is implemented.

Program is evaluated annually.

FLOWCHART II

15

# CHAPTER FIVE

## POINTS OF CONCERN

The first area of concern (interaction among educators, parents, students, and other community members), will have initially been addressed as a part of the policy development. Continued interaction will be an essential and natural result of an effective program.

The second point, interaction between an educator or a concerned staff person and a "troubled" student, is of primary importance if the program is going to be of value. Fortunately, educators and other concerned staff persons are in a unique position to observe students in a variety of settings. Thus, following staff inservice training they will quickly be able to zero in on those cases where assistance is called for. Anywhere students are — in classes, hallways, lunchrooms, formal and informal school social functions — concerned staff people need to be alert for trouble signs. Formal training should have provided educators with a review of normal adolescent behavior. Behavior of concern will be easily spotted, as will sudden changes in students whose behavior was acceptable before.

Behaviors of concern include, but are not limited to, absenteeism, tardiness, change in grades, change in extracurricular participation, withdrawal from or aggressiveness towards peers, lack of attention or falling asleep in class, or a hostile attitude toward teachers. Obvious physical signs such as bloodshot eyes, stumbling, or slurred speech would generate concern. Very often the behavior which triggers concern is also interfering in the academic, social, personal, or physical growth and performance of a student.

It is clearly the right and responsibility of the concerned educator to discuss such behaviors with students. The difficulty often arises in "knowing what to say." Perhaps the key to unlocking this difficulty is simple and honest feedback. Directly expressing concern to a student about the observed behavior is the most appropriate response. In this way, many students will receive assistance which will nurture their development and reduce the risk of future problems. We know that many adolescent problems can and will be resolved because of the concern and honest feedback shown by professional educators. The earlier we show this concern the greater the chance of resolving the problem at this initial intervention.

In some cases, student concerns and problems may not be resolved by communication with concerned educators or staff members. They may discover a complex and serious problem they are not qualified to handle, or they may be confronted by an angry, upset, or uncooperative student who chooses not to respond. Crucial to an effective student assistance program are structured procedures for staff to follow when referring students for further assessment and assistance (Point of Concern #3). Staff members must be confident that the procedures are logical, legal, and helpful.

In many cases, staff members are reluctant to get involved in this process fearing the lack of knowledge about specific youth problems (i.e., sexual, familial, chemical, legal, etc.) and their legal liability for doing something wrong. These concerns can be set aside if a specific procedure is outlined for staff to construct a profile of behaviors indicating a developing problem. Behaviors such as poor attendance, tardiness, lack of attention, deteriorating physical appearance, acting out in class, a drop in grades, and dropping out of extracurricular activities should be documented. It is interesting to note the behaviors listed are educational concerns related to the teaching/learning process and well within the legal bounds for any staff person to respond to independent of extensive training or knowledge of specific youth problems. Legal and professional questions can be raised only when teachers and other staff persons make assumptions as to the *cause* of certain behaviors; or react to rumors and hearsay, not identifiable behavior.

18

## Procedures Which Will Clarify Concerned Teacher's Role

1. Identify a student assistance preassessment person or team to receive referrals.
2. Develop a referral form for teachers which will elicit specific observations.
3. Familiarize all staff with the student assistance preassessment person(s), the referral form(s), and an overview of the services.

The teacher can quickly and easily make a referral if it is called for. After the referral has been made, the next concern is the interaction between the student assistance preassessment person and the student.

The focus of this interaction (Point of Concern #4) should be student-centered with the primary goal to provide assistance to the student. Discipline cannot be the only purpose of this process if the goal of the program is to help students. Disciplinary action, when indicated, should be administered *in conjunction with* the student assistance program. Focusing on needs and concerns of the student will help the student realize the program is designed to help him/her attain personal goals. It is important to note that focusing on the student's personal needs and concerns can also shift emphasis from the area of concern identified by the referring staff member. The preassessment staff person must be open to negotiation and to cooperatively establish goals the student identifies as significant. Remember — the goal of this program is to assist students; therefore, students must be directly involved in identifying specific areas which are troublesome to them. Through goal setting, students will be encouraged to accept responsibility for their own behavior; this also enables the preassessment staff person to provide specific assistance to each troubled student.

After goals are determined, the preassessment staff person may want to seek the advice and counsel of other preassessment staff (Point of Concern #5). Professional cooperation and collaboration will generally improve the assistance provided students. Professional discussion regarding specific assistance to be provided to a student should be a consistent component of the program. Recommendations can then be made to the student to help him/her achieve those predetermined goals (Point of Concern #6).

It should be noted that, in many cases, only minimal consultation with other support staff will be necessary. However, on occasion it may be necessary to involve a school nurse, counselor, social worker, psychologist, and/or a police liaison officer to develop an action plan that will truly benefit the troubled student. The action plan may call for assistance from community human service agencies as well as existing school resources. Often, a combination of the two will prove the most beneficial.

The Program Framework Flowchart II alerts you to set up "cooperative relationships with local public and private helping agencies." It is the responsibility of the preassessment staff person or team to be current with the resources available to determine the most appropriate resource for specific services. The school should neither provide diagnostic services nor function as a treatment program for serious chemical use. It also should not attempt to solve emotional, sexual, medical, or legal problems. Thus, a cooperative relationship with other agencies is imperative to the success of the program.

Fortunately, most adolescent problems can be resolved within the school community, utilizing the various skills of the staff, parents, and other students. Personal skills and strengths of school community members should be identified so that students can rely as much as possible on existing school resources.

Flowchart III is designed to give you an overview of the student assistance program procedures we have explained.

If the problem identified by the student and the preassessment staff warrants a diagnostic evaluation or therapy outside the school, it will be necessary to assist the student when he/she returns to school. The transition may be difficult for the student, his/her friends, and teachers. Both peer support and

# STUDENT ASSISTANCE PROCESS

FLOWCHART III

**Student Behavior of Concern**

**Concerned School Staff Member Response**

**Pre-Assessment**

**GOALS**

**Action Plan**

**Referral to Community Resources**

**Referral to Existing School Resources**

**ON-GOING SUPPORT**

21

counseling (individual and/or group) may be required to help the student avoid a return to problematic behavior.

Let us stress once again, the overall goal of the program is to assist troubled students. This can be successfully accomplished if the six points of concern we have defined are met.

# CHAPTER SIX

# ROLES AND RESPONSIBILITIES

## Administrator's Role and Responsibilities

The administration must be involved from the outset, either collectively or through a key administrator delegated to work on the task force responsible for the development of the school student assistance program policy. This policy should address a wide range of issues: prevention, early problem identification, referral procedures, legal questions, medical emergencies, treatment programs, school reentry programs, and staff training.

The administration's overt as well as subtle support of these policy program efforts is absolutely necessary to the success of the program. In many cases, administration must not only allow for but be directly responsible for

a. necessary staff training;
b. meetings among community members and staff with community resources;
c. clerical staff to produce referral forms and to disseminate program information;
d. program evaluation, tabulation, and dissemination;
e. program changes as indicated by evaluations;
f. liaison between board of education members and the rest of the student assistance program team.

## Teacher's Role and Responsibilities

**1.** Observe/Identify Behavior of Concern

We must assume that every teacher is a potential "concerned staff member," i.e., the one who recognizes and formally notes the aberrant or suddenly-changed behavior of a particular student. It is important to remember that the simple identification of problem behavior is all that is asked of this teacher; in fact, it is all that is wanted. Making assumptions about or diagnosing the "cause" of certain behaviors is definitely not called for.

**2.** Document

To be more specific, what this staff member is asked to do is record

    **a.** absenteeism

    **b.** tardiness

    **c.** diminishing quality of assignments

    **d.** trouble with peers

    **e.** hostility toward staff members

    **f.** changes in appearance

    **g.** changes in after school activities

    **h.** any other changes that compel attention

**3.** Share Concern

If problem behaviors persist for more than a week (or whatever length of time program procedures specify), this concerned staff member should bring the noted changes in behavior to the attention of the student, always express personal concern, and offer to help.

**4.** Refer

If this honest, specific feedback elicits no changed behavior, the concerned staff member should fill out a referral form (see Sample Materials, Chapter VIII), thus bringing the student and the problem to the attention of a student assistance preassessment team member.

We recommend communication procedures (consistent with federal and state confidentiality and data privacy laws) be established between the school and the various resources working with students. The concerned staff member may then be apprised of any information that would enhance involvement with the student.

### The Student Assistance Preassessment Team's Responsibility

The team, in cooperation with the task force and the school administration, will be generally responsible for implementing the procedures determined for the specific program. Close cooperation and communication among team members are essential to effective implementation. Specifically, the team will

a. respond to referrals from teachers and other school staff;
b. assess the nature and the extent of the problem;
c. make appropriate referrals to existing school programs/persons or to community resources such as social service agencies or treatment programs;
d. provide follow-up by monitoring the student's progress in the program referred to;
e. communicate to teachers and administrators the progress of the student, respecting federal and state confidentiality and data privacy laws;
f. monitor the program's effectiveness with individual cases.

The major goal of the preassessment process is to determine the most appropriate resource for helping a student resolve his or her concerns. The following model describes a process of selecting the least restrictive response to the student's problem.

The training needs of the program team members will vary according to the training and experience of individual members. The following opportunities should be offered to all team members to

1. develop or review group membership and working compatibility;
2. contact and assess community agencies and resources;
3. develop one-to-one communication skills;
4. develop skills in family intervention;
5. develop skills in conducting effective inservice training.

In summary, the school's role in assisting students is multifaceted, with administrators, individual teachers, and program team members all contributing services designed to help troubled students find solutions to their problems.

# A MODEL FOR MATCHING STUDENT NEEDS
## WITH SCHOOL AND COMMUNITY RESOURCES

| | LOW LEVEL OF PROBLEM SEVERITY | HIGH LEVEL OF PROBLEM SEVERITY |
|---|---|---|
| **HIGH LEVEL OF SOCIAL SUPPORT AND DEVELOPMENTAL COMPETENCY** | **A** A response which focuses on information or education which the student needs to change behavior. | **C** A response which provides some sort of low structured program of treatment or remediation. |
| **LOW LEVEL OF SOCIAL SUPPORT AND DEVELOPMENTAL COMPETENCY** | **B** A response which focuses on life skills, social competencies or social support which the student needs to change behavior. | **D** A response which provides a highly structured program of treatment or remediation. |

Ron Brand
St. Paul, MN

26

# CHAPTER SEVEN

## PROBLEM PREVENTION:
## DIRECTION FOR THE FUTURE

As we have demonstrated, student assistance programs are designed to quickly and efficiently direct students to the help needed to handle their problems so they can become productive again. However, it is surely the hope of all of us that we can begin to influence young people's lives enough to prevent at least some problems from occurring rather than always being in the position of helping students find solutions.

It is our belief that both elementary and secondary educators, and all others who participate in the education continuum, can and should assume significant roles in the area of prevention.

Many prevention efforts can be easily undertaken. A prerequisite is commitment, as quality educators demonstrate from the moment they make their career choice. The efforts listed here are essential if we want to have a positive influence on the direction of our young people's lives.

**A.** Develop a caring school climate.

**B.** Provide instruction and experience in decision-making.

**C.** Help each person understand his/her individual uniqueness and worth.

**D.** Provide varied outlets for student self-development and creativity.

**E.** Provide information about
1. chemicals and chemical use in our society;
2. human sexuality and sexual behavior in our society;
3. legal rights and responsibilities;
4. personal and community health.

**F.** Provide opportunities to develop group participation skills.

**G.** Provide athletic and other cocurricular activities as an opportunity to discuss health issues and concerns.

In cooperation with the family, schools can help children learn and develop personal strengths and social skills which will enable them to make responsible decisions both personally and socially.

It is important to address both prevention specifics and health promotion concerns within the broad area of prevention. Efforts that focus only on preventing a specific problem *will not be successful* if the elimination of that problem also eliminates the sought-after positive feelings and satisfaction. For example, the irresponsible use of alcohol is both problematic to a young person and the source of excitement, status, peer acceptance, and self-enhancement. Thus, efforts to prevent the irresponsible use of alcohol must also be accompanied by involvement in activities that provide a source of personal satisfaction. Educators need to promote health and at the same time prevent specific youth problems. To be effective, prevention efforts and health promotion must be integrated into existing programs. Prevention must be recognized as a developmental process which occurs slowly, reflecting the influence of family, friends, and community as well as teachers. Prevention is not something that occurs for twenty minutes on Monday, Wednesday, and Friday.

Student assistance is a big challenge offered to educators, not unlike the challenges their students face while trying to grow comfortably from childhood to adulthood. Concern, cooperation, and commitment are required. As educators, we are in a unique position to effect healthy changes in our society by effecting healthy changes in the lives of all the students who pass through our classrooms. It's a big job and one we all need help with. It is our hope that the program we have outlined in these pages will help each of you better meet the needs of the "troubled students," who are our shared responsibility.

# CHAPTER EIGHT

## SAMPLE MATERIALS

The sample materials have been included to assist you in the various phases of your policy and program development. They are offered as guidelines, subject to whatever changes might be necessary to better tailor them to your own school or district.

**A.** Administrator's checklist of "things to be done" after the decision to develop the policy has been made.

**B.** Brief overview of the major activities in program development.

**C.** Awareness training workshop models for parents, staff, and community.

**D.** Agency referral checklist.

**E.** Suggested referral form that may be used by concerned staff when referring a troubled student to a preassessment person.

**F.** Two actual policies and programs which were designed to fit the needs of specific school districts.

## A.

### Administrator's Checklist

This checklist briefly designates necessary items to be handled by the core of persons involved in the development of both the policy and the program. We want to stress that this checklist is not all-inclusive. However, it will provide you with a place to begin. We suggest that you designate a person responsible for carrying out each of the particular tasks as quickly as possible. Experience also taught us that determining a time line for completion kept the process moving and kept all the participants current with the tasks yet to be completed.

# I. Administrative Concerns and Questions That Each School Board or Governing Body Needs to Address:

**A.** Identification of person(s) responsible for assessing, planning, implementing, and evaluating program efforts, recognizing the complexities of chemical use problems and the varying expertise of individuals.

    **1.** Has an ongoing advisory group or task force made up of administrators*, teachers*, parents*, students*, professional and support staff*, chemical dependency/health professionals, maintenance and service personnel, and community leaders been organized? (While all of the people listed above are appropriate, those marked with an asterisk are essential.)

    **2.** Have building resource persons been identified to respond to crisis intervention situations?

    **3.** Have staff resource persons with professional training and appropriate experience been identified in each building to respond to student chemical use problems?

    **4.** Has someone been assigned responsibility for the coordination and development of alcohol and other drug abuse prevention curriculum K-9?

**B.** Systematic assessment of needs of school community for prevention, intervention, and aftercare support.

    **1.** Assessment of the needs of the school community.

        **a.** Have school policies and procedures been written or revised to reflect changes in state or federal law?

        **b.** Have school policies and procedures for responding to student problems, i.e., chemical use, child abuse and neglect, discipline, been integrated where appropriate?

        **c.** Have the different roles and responsibilities of school staff in the minimization of chemical use problems been clearly defined and communicated?

    **d.** Have provisions been made to allow students to maintain academic progress while participating in a therapeutic treatment program?

    **e.** Have procedures been developed to allow students and staff to participate in support groups during the regular school schedule?

**2.** Assessment of resources available within the school.

    **a.** Have all school staff been trained in chemical use problem prevention and intervention?

    **b.** Have selected staff members received specialized training in chemical use problem prevention and intervention?

    **c.** Are these special staff being used effectively?

    **d.** Are special services within the district, i.e., special education, social work, counseling, and health care currently available to students?

**3.** Assessment of the community resources available to the school.

    **a.** Have cooperative relationships been established with existing public helping agencies — city, county, state, and federal?

    **b.** Have cooperative relationships been established with local law enforcement agencies?

    **c.** Is the listing of the private human service organizations available to the school district updated annually?

    **d.** Are the locations, dates, and phone numbers for Al-Anon, Alateen, and other support groups available to all students and staff?

**C.** Establishment of an ongoing evaluation and assessment process to promote appropriate programming and insure flexibility of procedures.

**1.** Are the district policy and procedures reviewed regularly?

**2.** Is the alcohol and other drug education curriculum K-12 regularly reviewed and revised?

**3.** Is an annual review of critical incidents, procedures, and referrals conducted?

## II. Training to Insure That All Staff Have the Knowledge and Skills to Implement Efforts to Minimize Chemical Use Problems Among Students:

**A.** Are all staff aware of the school's responsibility to respond to student chemical use problems?

**B.** Have all school staff been made aware of chemical use and related problems and the specific purposes of prevention, intervention, therapy, and aftercare?

**C.** Have appropriate staff received information related to existing state laws, policies and procedures for preventing and responding to student problems, i.e., chemical use, child abuse and neglect, and discipline?

**D.** Have prevention curriculum and instruction skills for appropriate staff been developed?

**E.** Has each staff member's responsibility and liability in responding to student problems, i.e., chemical use, child abuse and neglect, and discipline been clarified?

**F.** Have all staff had an opportunity to develop the skills to observe and report specific and identifiable behaviors of concern?

**G.** Are all staff aware of the needs of students either returning to school after completing therapy/treatment or currently involved in outpatient therapy?

## III. A Summary of the Prevention and Health Promoting Questions Each School Board or Other Governing Body Should Consider:

**A.** Have efforts been made to establish a caring school community with empathy, compassion, and communication extended among administrators, students, teachers, and parents?

32

**B.** Have efforts been made to establish an emotionally healthy classroom which includes emphasis on development of a positive self-concept, coping skills, interpersonal relationships, decision-making, and assertiveness?

**C.** Has a K-12 comprehensive health curriculum been established which includes emphasis on health promotion and chemical health issues?

**D.** Has pharmacological information been integrated into the K-12 curriculum appropriate to the student's age and environment? This should include specific information on the effects of chemical use on athletic and other activity performance.

**E.** Have prevention concepts and strategies been integrated into all curriculum areas?

**F.** Have the unique needs of students experiencing family problems, i.e., chemical use, child abuse and neglect, or family change been recognized?

**G.** Have support groups been established to provide students and staff the opportunity to examine personal chemical use patterns?

**H.** Has the school district made efforts to establish programs to improve parent/student communication?

**I.** Has the district established or promoted programs in parenting skills for students and adults?

**J.** Does the district provide a healthy balance of extracurricular and cocurricular activities which allows student self-development and creativity, recognizing individual needs, interests, and skill levels?

## IV. A Summary of the Intervention Questions Each School Board or Other Governing Body Should Consider:

**A.** Has the district developed procedures to follow when a student seeks help or when a staff member or student observes individual behavior which indicates a chemical use problem?

**B.** Has the district developed procedures to follow when a staff member or student uses chemicals inappropriately or illegally while on school property or attending school functions? These procedures should follow due process and include provisions for
  1. education regarding chemical use problems;
  2. preassessment interview;
  3. disciplinary actions.
**C.** Has the district developed procedures for involving school personnel with a family or student troubled by chemical use problems?
**D.** Has the district developed a process to communicate with treatment or therapeutic programs regarding student needs and progress in accordance with existing state and federal confidentiality laws?
**E.** Has the district developed chemical use problem crisis intervention procedures to respond to medical emergencies, i.e., overdose or withdrawal?
**F.** Has the district developed procedures for transfer of persons to detoxification facilities?
**G.** Has the district developed procedures to follow when a student is behaving in ways which may cause him/her or others harm?
**H.** Has the district developed procedures to notify the local county welfare department or law enforcement agent immediately when abuse or neglect is suspected?
**I.** Has a group support system been established for individuals returning to the school community after completing therapy/treatment for chemical use problems?
**J.** Have cooperative relationships been established with community resources to help students who are returning to the school community after completing therapy/treatment?
**K.** Have provisions been made for special tutoring service when needed?

**L.** Have provisions been made, in accordance with existing state and federal confidentiality laws, to maintain communication with therapeutic/treatment programs regarding student needs and progress upon returning to school?

## B.

### Student Assistance Program
### from Inception to Implementation: A Brief Overview

School A — The principal of a small rural secondary school became concerned over the apparent misuse of chemicals by students in school and during extracurricular school activities. After attending a number of workshops and meetings with various state, school, and community persons, it was decided to initiate a student assistance program. A task force made up of the principal, secondary counselor, school board member, parent, two students (one junior and one senior), and four teachers (Physical Education, Math, Health Education, and English) was selected to plan and develop a local program.

The task force met for one full day to begin the task of developing a program that would be appropriate for the local district. By the end of the day, the framework for writing a school policy was developed together with a plan for obtaining future input from the teaching staff, school board, and student council. The group met several times after school to work on the specific components of the policy and for a half day prior to submitting a rough draft of the policy to the staff, board of education, and student council. Specific procedures were in place and community resources were identified. After reviewing the input from the groups involved, a number of changes were made and the policy was ready for board of education approval.

The board of education approved the policy and it was ready for implementation. A half-day inservice workshop was scheduled for all staff; the policy was printed in the student handbook and the community was informed via the local media.

The entire process of developing this program took approximately a year and a half from beginning to implementation. This program has now expanded and is providing prevention efforts K-12.

## C.

### Sample Workshops Designed to Enhance Program Effectiveness

After recognizing the need, and developing a policy and a set of procedures that reflect unique needs, interests, and resources of the local school community, it is necessary to develop a plan to disseminate information and provide awareness inservice training for those people affected by the student assistance program. School staff, parents, students, and community agency personnel are likely to be the primary audience for awareness training.

The development of the program and the awareness training plan must reflect unique school community characteristics along with needs and interests of each group. To assist in this process, we have outlined awareness training workshop models including suggested objectives.

*Parent Awareness Workshop*
Goal:

To inform parents of the purpose and functioning of the student assistance program and increase cooperation between the school and the home. As a result of the session, parents will be able to
1. explain the purpose of the school student assistance program;
2. identify student assistance assessment staff at their school and know how to contact the staff;
3. discuss the purpose and specific procedures of the student assistance program with other parents and their children.

Format:

A two-hour evening session which includes brief lectures about the purpose and procedures of the student assistance program; distribution of the school student assistance policy, and opportunities to discuss feelings and thoughts regarding the policy and program procedures.

Agenda:

  **I.** Introduction of the Student Assistance Program Parent Awareness Workshop by
    — school principal;
    — representative of parents' association;
    — parent involved in developing the program.
     **a.** goal of program
     **b.** development of the program
  **II.** Small group discussion of key issues regarding student problems and the school's response.
  **III.** Overview of student assistance program. Use flowchart provided or develop a local flowchart.
  **IV.** Question and answer session.
  **V.** Opportunity for written comments (suggested topics for evaluative comments).
    **1.** Strengths of program
    **2.** Points of personal concern
    **3.** Suggestions for improving program
  **VI.** Summary.

*Staff Inservice Training*

Goal:

To inform school staff of the purpose and functioning of the student assistance program and to instruct school staff in the specific procedures to be followed.

As a result of the session(s) school staff will be able to

  **1.** explain the purpose of the school student assistance program;
  **2.** identify student assistance program assessment staff at their school;

3. express feelings of concern to students regarding specific student behaviors;
4. utilize referral forms appropriately.
5. Discuss the purpose and specific procedures of the student assistance program with colleagues, parents, and students.

Format:
   A four-hour session conducted during the regularly-scheduled teacher day, which includes brief lectures about the purpose and procedures of the student assistance program, distribution of the student assistance program policy, referral flowchart and referral forms, and opportunities to discuss feelings and thoughts regarding the student assistance program.

Agenda:
   I. Introduction of the Student Assistance Program School Staff Workshop by
      — school principal;
      — coordinator of student assistance program.
         a. goal of program
         b. development of program
   II. Small group discussion of key issues regarding student problems and the school's response.
   III. Overview of student assistance program procedures
         a. flowchart
         b. distribute local policy and procedures to participants.
   IV. Determining behaviors of concern.
   V. Small group discussion of sample case studies.
   VI. Presentation of local in-school programs and community agencies to be utilized by student assistance assessment staff.
   VII. Total group question/answer session.
   VIII. Opportunity for written comments from school staff members on points of concern, problems and strengths.
   IX. Summary

*Community Agency Personnel Awareness Workshop*

Goal:

To inform community agency staff of the purpose and functioning of the student assistance program and to increase the level of cooperation and collaboration between the school and community agencies. As a result of the session, participants will be able to

1. explain the purpose of the school student assistance program;
2. identify student assistance program assessment staff at the school;
3. define the role of their agencies in responding to the problems of youth referred to their agency;
4. recognize and utilize referral and communication forms provided by the school;
5. discuss the purpose and specific procedures of the student assistance program with colleagues, school staff, parents, and students.

Format:

A two-hour session which includes brief lectures and activities designed to 1) explain the purpose of the program, referral forms, and procedures, and 2) provide an opportunity to discuss feelings and thoughts about the program.

Agenda:

**I.** Introduction of the Student Assistance Program School Staff Workshop by
— school principal
— coordinator of student assistance program
   **a.** goal of program
   **b.** development of program
**II.** Small group discussion of key issues regarding student problems and the school's response.
**III.** Overview of student assistance program procedures
   **a.** distribute flowchart
   **b.** distribute local policy and procedures to participants

**IV.** Determining problematic behaviors.
**V.** Small group discussion of sample case studies.
**VI.** Presentation of local in-school programs and community agencies to be utilized by student assistance staff.
**VII.** Total group question/answer session.
**VIII.** Opportunity for written comments from school staff members on points of concern, problems and strengths.
**IX.** Summary.

## D.

### Issues To Consider When Making Agency Referrals

In referring a student to a community agency for assessment, diagnosis, or treatment, it is important to match student needs with agency goals, methods, resources, and successes. The following questions will be helpful in determining the appropriateness of a specific agency for a particular student and his or her problem.

1. What is the agency's goal or purpose?
2. What types of service does the agency provide?
3. Who is eligible to receive services from the agency?
4. What type of client is most successful in using the agency's services?
5. How does the agency measure success?
6. How are clients accepted for services?
7. How long are clients involved in receiving services?
8. Are family members of the client involved in the services? If so, to what extent?
9. What is the agency policy for communicating with school staff about student clients?
10. Are aftercare and long-term support services provided?
11. What are the qualifications and experience of professional staff?

12. What are the costs for each type of service? Is the agency eligible for third party reimbursement?
13. Are the agency facilities accessible to the client?

## E.

### Suggested Referral Form

The _____ school Student Assistance Program is intended to systematically and professionally respond to the problems of students. This referral form is intended to provide school staff an opportunity to involve a student, demonstrating problematic behavior, with our program assessment team so that his/her problems might be resolved.

Please complete this form as accurately and thoroughly as you can. The information you provide may be shared with the student and his/her parents at the professional discretion of the program assessment team.

Thank you for your cooperation and concern.

List specific student behavior which seems problematic to you. Be as specific as possible:

*Behavior*                    *Location*                    *Time & Date*

List specific actions which you have taken in response to these behaviors:

|  |  |  | *Student's Response* |
| *Your Action* | *Location* | *Time & Date* | *To Your Action* |

## F.

### Policies & Programs

Throughout the state, chemical use and abuse among young people has attracted the attention of parents and educators alike. Because of their concern, frequent requests for help have been made to the Minnesota Department of Education. Our response as prevention specialists led to numerous schools and districts forming policies and programs addressing chemical use as a major problem area. Thus, both policies and programs shared with you here focus on chemical use as the student problem of concern for which assistance was needed.

However, as educators, we realize that chemical use may only be a symptom of other problems that also deserve assistance. As we stated in the introduction, the employee assistance programs which successfully operate in major firms and organizations nationwide served as a model for the development of the policies and programs that we guided. In turn, it is our belief that from these samples you can easily develop a more inclusive program able to assist students with any number of problems.

The school or district size is a factor of concern when planning your policy and accompanying program. Thus, we chose as samples a large district and a very small one. These should illustrate that however great or limited your resources may seem, a program can be designed that will be helpful to all concerned in the school, home, and community.

The first program (School District A), was planned for four school districts in a rural setting. The combined student population was approximately 5,500 in grades K-12.

## School District "A"

## POLICY STATEMENT

### Student Assistance Program

Many students are troubled by problems which interfere, not only with their academic and cocurricular performance, but with their emotional, physical, mental, and social development as well. The main goal of the Student Assistance Program is to systematically and professionally respond to students' problems as they are manifested in school. The Student Assistance Program will provide a structured, organized approach to all schools within the district to offer assistance to students troubled by physical, emotional, social, legal, sexual, medical, familial, or chemical use problems. It will also provide a structured, organized liaison between the school and outside agencies. This would include monitoring the educational program of students in a treatment facility and assisting in the adjustment of the student returning from an outside placement.

1. This policy does not alter or replace existing administrative policy, disciplinary procedures, contractual agreements, or state law, but serves to assist in their utilization.
2. The policy applies to all students.
3. Students will be encouraged to seek assistance to determine if personal problems are causing unsatisfactory academic or cocurricular performance. If performance problems are corrected, no further action will be taken.
4. It is the intent of the Student Assistance Program to work cooperatively with parents and guardians to resolve student problems. Parents and guardians will be contacted as soon as possible when appropriate.
5. All records and discussions of personal problems will be handled in a confidential manner. These records will be kept at the designated counseling resource, and will not become a part of the student's cumulative file.
6. The program provides for preliminary assessment of student problems and referral, if appropriate. Costs for diagnostic and treatment services outside the school are the responsibility of parents or guardians.

This policy recognizes the responsibility of the school in responding to student problems. The school also recognizes its role and responsibility to prevent problems and promote health as part of a comprehensive program.

This program, School District "B," is designed for a community of 30,000 which is part of a metropolitan area, the home of some higher education institutions. The population of the total area exceeds 100,000. The total student population is 5,289 in grades K-12.

# School District "B"

## Chemical Use Philosophy & Policy

It is our goal to create a caring atmosphere for each student within the system. It is recognized that this caring environment is the first step in preventing an individual from becoming harmfully involved with chemicals. This prevention is instituted by nurturing successful interpersonal relationships and promoting skills in decision making and problem solving, while providing for students' academic growth.

In spite of such efforts, the district understands that a student may become harmfully involved with some chemical. This involvement would create pain for themselves and/or others. At this juncture, the school must continue to operate as a caring rather than a punitive community. The harmfully involved individual will be assisted in seeking supportive and rehabilitative services, without fear of penalty. If treatment becomes necessary outside the school setting, every effort must be exerted to effect a successful continuation in/or reentry into the school setting.

The Board of Education endorses this philosophy built upon prevention, identification of the harmfully involved, appropriate intervention with provision for support services, and the continuation of staff training.

The administration is charged to implement this policy through procedures to provide for the following:
  I. Prevention
 II. Procedures in the Helping Process
    a. identification of harmfully involved students
    b. determination of the problem
III. Immediate Intervention
 IV. Support Services
  V. Staff Training

# PREVENTION

Prevention will be directed toward providing students with information and developmental experiences which will enable them to make responsible decisions regarding chemical usage.

**A.** Prevention merits developing a comprehensive and coordinated program which includes
1. pharmacological information appropriate to the student's age and development which includes potential social, psychological, and physical effects of chemicals;
2. understanding peer pressures and the influences upon students' lives coupled with a comprehension of the effects of emotions and stress in students' lives.

**B.** Effective communication is instrumental in this type of prevention throughout all levels of the educational institution. Most important is an emotionally healthy classroom which daily encourages the following:
1. positive self-concept;
2. enthusiasm for learning;
3. outlets for self-development and creativity which acknowledge individual skill levels, needs, and interests;
4. responsible decision making and problem solving;
5. recognition of special needs identified with high-risk students or families experiencing undue stress.

**C.** Prevention of harmful chemical involvement includes helping parents and community to be aware of
1. family communication — parenting;
2. child growth and development;
3. understanding peer pressure;
4. value conflicts and problem solving;
5. early signals of drug usage;
6. knowledge and value of support groups.

# PROCEDURES IN THE HELPING PROCESS

Identification of the harmfully involved students.

**A.** Teacher and/or Facilitator

1. The teacher has the most contact with a student and is, therefore, in the best position to observe any significant change in a student's behavior. These changes may provide an index of changes in a student's lifestyle. At all times, the teacher should focus upon observable behavior.

   **a.** The teacher will document absenteeism, poor performance, sickness, negative personality changes, or peculiar behavior.

   **b.** The teacher and other school personnel will discuss these behaviors with the student. No evaluation is involved at this juncture.

2. Should a student not respond positively to the abovementioned encounter, the following measures may be pursued:

   **a.** A review of the *consequences* of a student's behavior will be done by either the instructor or facilitator. It will be highlighted that the student is responsible for his/her behavior.

   **b.** Time will be given for a student to improve his/her behavior. The teacher/facilitator involved will document this action.

3. If the student's performance and behavior *do not* improve to an acceptable level, either the teacher or facilitator will

   **a.** discuss the performance again with the student;

   **b.** contact the parents or guardians of the child;

   **c.** the parents, teacher, and facilitator together will determine what action will be taken to help the student.

**B.** Health Service Personnel

1. Observe student's poor health and/or problems related to chemical use.

2. Discuss situation with student and suggest where to get assistance. Contact facilitator and/or instructor if it is appropriate; and finally, notify the parents.

3. If student is not receptive to suggestions, health service personnel
   a. outline medical consequences of behavior to student;
   b. contact instructor or school facilitator who follows "A" above.
4. If student is receptive to suggestions, health service personnel
   a. contact facilitator and explain situation;
   b. set up student interview with facilitator;
   c. document action.
5. In emergencies, give care, refer directly to community resources, and notify administrator.

C. Student
1. discusses chemical dependency or related problems with instructor, health services personnel, or facilitator and asks for help.
2. is given suggestions where to get help and assistance in seeking help, if desired.
3. If student is not receptive to suggestions
   a. consequences of behavior are outlined — student is responsible for outcome;
   b. facilitator or health service personnel contact instructor as appropriate;
   c. person contacted may follow "A" above.
4. If student is receptive to suggestions
   a. consequences of behavior are outlined;
   b. instructor contacts facilitator, explains situation, sets up interview with facilitator (may accompany student), documents action;
   c. facilitator or health service personnel refer student to appropriate community resource for assistance (may accompany student), document action.

D. Principal
1. Student has violated school rule, State Department of Education regulations, and/or applicable state laws such as possession or use of alcohol or mood-altering drugs on

school premises. If deemed necessary will involve appropriate authority; i.e., police, probation officer, social worker.

2. An intervention meeting is held with concerned parties including the parents or guardians.
3. Student is offered options:
   a. seek diagnostic evaluation and recommendation by resource specialist for chemical dependency or related problems;
   b. dismissal under established procedures.
4. In an emergency case which requires immediate health services, the principal shall arrange follow-up.

Determination of Problem — When a student is referred to the building's facilitator, the facilitator interviews the student and identifies the nature of the problem.

A. The facilitator will determine probable harmful chemical involvement by establishing facts of chemical use and poor performance.
   1. Should the student prove receptive to suggestions, the facilitator
      a. has determined that the student's poor performance is probably a clue to his/her personal or family member's chemical use;
      b. refers the student to a community resource specialist for diagnostic evaluation and recommendation. The student is assured that he or she may re-enter school at an appropriate time, if inpatient treatment is indicated.
   2. The facilitator will contact specialist to obtain recommendations for the student. These may be as follows:
      a. Participate in sessions with a chemical dependency facilitator.
      b. Attend Alcoholics Anonymous, Narcotics Anonymous, or Alateen meetings.
      c. Go to an outpatient clinic or a hospital for detoxification.
      d. Enter a treatment facility.

**e.** Enter a hospital for detoxification.

**B.** After such action has been taken, it is necessary to continue to provide support.

1. The facilitator maintains contact with the resource to monitor the student's recovery. This information can be relayed only with a signed release.

2. If treatment has necessitated the student be placed in an alternative setting, it will be necessary for the facilitator to provide a supportive return to school.

3. Upon return to school, the facilitator works with the instructor(s) to check on progress. This should be documented.

4. Students who don't leave the school setting who receive treatment will receive continual support from the facilitator and instructors.

**C.** If student denies that chemicals are a problem and the facilitator suspects that they are, facilitator

1. sets up an intervention meeting for student with appropriate persons significant to the student present (may include instructor, health service personnel, family, and student);

2. conducts an intervention, confronting student with documented performance and its relation to chemical intake;

3. presents the following recommendation to the student:

**a.** go to community resource specialist for diagnostic evaluation and recommendations.

# IMMEDIATE INTERVENTION

Immediate intervention is merited whenever the behavior of a student jeopardizes his/her health, safety, or welfare or that of other students or staff. In addition, immediate intervention is mandated when a student is observed using mood-altering chemicals in violation of state or federal laws.

Should a student demonstrate behavior suggesting immediate danger to his/her health, the following action will be taken:

1. The staff member involved will secure whatever help is needed to provide first aid and to insure the well-being of others present.
2. Should the student's behavior indicate a potential over-dose or withdrawal, the staff should attempt to determine the type of drug taken.
   a. an inspection of the student's clothing or locker may be necessary;
   b. staff members will try to ask friends and associates of the student for information;
   c. careful observations will be made of any odors or types of behaviors displayed.
3. Parents will be contacted immediately, advised of the crisis situation and involved in action for the transfer of the student to a medical facility — if deemed necessary.
4. When parents cannot be contacted, the student will be transferred to a medical facility.
5. After the student's immediate needs have been attended to, planning with the student and parents will begin. This will provide for long-range planning to administer to the student's behavior within the school context as well as within the larger community.
   a. the student is to be held responsible for his/her actions;
   b. support is to be provided to help the student understand his/her behavior within the school and broader social context;

**c.** legal ramifications may be pursued at the discretion of the school or parents. It should be emphasized that this avenue would be pursued if it is believed to be helpful to the student.

## SUPPORT SERVICES

1. Cooperating with the treatment facility by providing information necessary to enable the facility to plan for the student's educational needs.
2. Reassuring the student that appropriate school credit will be given for the treatment experience.
3. Planning with the treatment facility so that progress made in treatment can be maintained once the student returns to the school environment.
4. Formulating a school schedule which will consider alternatives which best suit the student's ability to function (e.g., part-day schedule, credit for ongoing therapy, tutoring, etc.).
5. Preparing instructors to give support and approval through the State Department of Education to the student when he/she continues in or returns to class.
6. Instituting peer support groups directed at providing opportunities for new peer groups for students struggling to stay "straight." This support would offer a solid base from which the student can grow as an independent and responsible person.
7. Securing communication channels with home and community resources who provide support for positive growth.
8. Establishing support groups for students at all levels of chemical use:
   a. information group
   b. awareness group
   c. use group
   d. chemical dependency treatment group
9. Instructing students in accepting and offering support to students who have received treatment.

## STAFF TRAINING

In order to implement the prevention, intervention and after-care phases of the program, it is important that administration, plus full and part-time staff, be made aware of the part they can play in creating a caring and responsible school community. By cooperating with community resources, a successful training program can be accomplished. This training should focus upon the following components:

1. Training should include information which enhances staff awareness of various "patterns of use." This training would dictate inservice training annually, punctuated with periodic activities designed to strengthen staff knowledge and skills.

2. Fundamental to such training is an emphasis upon techniques that develop communication skills to encourage positive growth in students.

3. Cooperation with community resources such as media, churches, service organizations, colleges, and universities will enable a variety of programs to develop which can strengthen awareness and skills.

# Hazelden

*Other titles that will interest you...*

**What, When, and How to Talk to Students
about Alcohol and Other Drugs**
A Guide for Teachers
  *by Gail Gleason Milgram, Ed.D. and Thomas Griffin, M.S.W.*
  School teachers have unique opportunities to educate young people
about drinking and taking drugs. This book, an authoritative guide written by the author of *What, When, and How to Talk to Children about
Alcohol and other Drugs,* and the manager of Hazelden's Health Promotion Services, provides the guidelines and information necessary to
teach students how to make responsible decisions about alcohol and
other drug use. (67 pp.)
Order No. 5191A

**Paying the Price**
  *by Thomas M. Griffin, M.S.W.*
  Today, professional athletes and the young athletes who admire them
face many decisions about their health, performance, and alcohol or
other drug use. This pamphlet by the Manager of Hazelden•Cork
Sports Education and Training Program describes how alcohol and
other drug use can affect performance, attitude, teammates and
coaches. (24 pp.)
Order No. 1378B

**Health Choices**
  Adolescents take risks daily in areas such as chemical use, sexual experimentation, or automobile use: risks that can affect their immediate
health and safety. *Health Choices* is a six unit health/prevention teaching package designed specifically to help teachers have a positive impact
on the health decisions of junior and senior high school students. Each
unit is composed of activity lessons which teach students to identify feelings, interact with peers, and make important health decisions that will
affect them now and in the future.
Order No. 5595A

**For price and order information, please call one of our
Customer Service Representatives.**

**Hazelden Educational Materials**

**Pleasant Valley Road
Box 176
Center City, MN 55012-0176**

**(800) 328-9000**
(Toll Free. U.S. Only)
**(800) 257-0070**
(Toll Free. MN Only)
**(800) 328-0500**
(Toll Free. Film and Video
Orders. U.S. Only)
**(612) 257-4010**
(Alaska and Outside U.S.)